LOOKING BACK

CIVILISATIONS OF
PERU

BEFORE 1535

HAZEL MARY MARTELL

Evans

EVANS BROTHERS LIMITED

Evans Brothers Limited
2A Portman Mansions
Chiltern Street
London W1M 1LE

Editor: Nicola Barber
Designer: Neil Sayer
Picture research: Victoria Brooker
Maps: Nick Hawken
Production: Jenny Mulvanny

Consultant: Dr Karen Wise, Assistant Curator,
Department of Anthropology, Los Angeles County
Museum of Natural History

Printed in Spain by GRAFO, S.A.- Bilbao

British Library Cataloguing in Publication Data

Martell, Hazel Mary
  Civilisations of Peru: before 1535. -(Looking back)
  1. Peru - Civilization - Juvenile literature 2. Peru -
History - To 1535 - Juvenile literature
  I.Title
  985'.01

ISBN 0237518201

Acknowledgements

Cover (main and background image) Tony Morrison/South American Pictures **title page** Robert
Frerck/Robert Harding Picture Library **page 7** (top) Robert Harding Picture Library (bottom) Kimball
Morrison/South American Pictures **page 8** H. R. Dörig/Hutchison Library **page 9** South American
Pictures **page 10** Tony Morrison/South American Pictures **page 11** Walter Rawlings/Robert Harding
Picture Library **page 12** e.t. archive **page 13** (top) e.t. archive (bottom) H. R. Dörig/Hutchison Library
page 14 Edward Parker/Hutchison Library **page 15** H. R. Dörig/Hutchison Library **page 17** George
Rainbird Ltd/Robert Harding Picture Library **page 18** e.t. archive **page 19** Tony Morrison/South
American Pictures **page 21** N. J Saunders/Werner Forman Archive **page 22** H. R. Dörig/Hutchison
Library **page 23** Tony Morrison/South American Pictures **page 24** Tony Morrison/South American
Pictures **page 25** Kimball Morrison/South American Pictures **page 27** Robert Frerck/Robert Harding
Picture Library **page 28** (top) Hutchison Library (bottom) D. F. E. Russell/Robert Harding Picture
Library **page 30** Werner Forman Archive **page 31** South American Pictures **page 32** Robert Harding
Picture Library **page 33** South American Pictures **page 34** Tony Morrison/South American Pictures
page 36 Robert Harding Picture Library **page 37 - 39** Werner Forman **page 40** Tony Morrison/South
American Pictures **page 41** H. R. Dörig/Hutchison Library **page 43** Tony Morrison/South American
Pictures **page 45** (top) Tony Morrison/South American Pictures (bottom) Peter Ryley/South American
Pictures **page 46** H. R. Dörig/Hutchison Library **page 47** (top) Werner Forman Archive (bottom) H. R.
Dörig/Hutchison Library **page 48** Tony Morrison/South American Pictures **page 50 - 53** Werner
Forman Archive **page 54** e.t. archive **page 57** South American Pictures **page 58** South American
Pictures **page 59** Tony Morrison/South American Pictures

CONTENTS

INTRODUCTION

This map shows the huge area covered by the Inca Empire at the time of the Spanish invasion in 1532.

Map labels: COLOMBIA, Quito, ECUADOR, Tumbes, BRAZIL, Cajamarca, PERU, Lima, Vilcabamba, Machu Picchu, Cuzco, Lake Titicaca, Pacific Ocean, BOLIVIA, CHILE, ARGENTINA, ANDES MOUNTAINS, N

Key

☐ Extent of Inca Empire in 1532

■ Present-day city

0 — 500 miles
0 — 500 km

Although this book has the title 'Peru before 1535', it actually examines a much larger area in South America than the country we know today as Peru. It looks at the huge territory covered by the Inca Empire at the time of the Spanish invasion in 1532. This empire included parts of what are now Ecuador, Bolivia, Argentina and Chile as well as modern-day Peru. Even in the centuries before the Incas gained control over the vast territories of their empire, these areas were linked by having similar cultures.

This region of South America is one of a startling variety of landscapes and climates. Along the Pacific coast runs a narrow strip of desert, dry and arid except where it is crossed by fertile river valleys. Rising dramatically from the desert are the Andes, some of the highest mountains in the world. Many of their topmost peaks are permanently covered in snow and ice. Other features of the mountains include

INTRODUCTION

glaciers and volcanoes, while earthquakes and tremors often shake the area. In between the mountain ranges lie areas of high plain, known as *altiplano*. They are covered in bleak, treeless grassland, called *puna*. The lower slopes of the mountains are forested, especially on the eastern side where the rainfall is heaviest. To the east of the Andes lies the great Amazon basin, a vast area of tropical rainforest.

Today, the coastal desert of Peru is crossed from north to south by the Pan American Highway, but it is still a bleak and inhospitable area.

The valley of Callejon de Huaylas in the west of central Peru is overlooked by the Cordillera Blanca, a range of mountains containing some of the country's highest peaks.

The dry atmosphere of the coastal desert has helped to preserve artefacts such as this embroidered panel. Made by the Paracas people (see pages 16-18), it is part of a large piece of cloth which was wrapped around a dead person before burial.

A CLOSER LOOK

When the Spaniards arrived, the Incas spoke a language called Quechua. Because this language had never been written down, the Spaniards used their own spellings for the names of people and places, based on what they heard. However, there are now attempts to simplify the spellings of Inca words. This means that in some books you will see, for example, Inca written as Inka, Huari written as Wari, and Tiahuanaco written as Tiwanaku.

CIVILISATIONS AND CONQUEST

Different cultures developed in this vast region at different times and archaeologists recognise many civilisations in the 3000-year period from 1400 BC to AD 1600. In chronological order, the most important are the Chavin, the Paracas, the Nazca, the Moche, the Tiahuanaco, the Huari, the Chimu and, finally, the Inca. They all have many things in common, especially in their arts and crafts, their gods, their architecture, their farming methods and their trading patterns. Some, such as the Chimu and the Inca, developed independently at more or less the same time as each other but none of them developed directly out of what had gone before. This book looks at each of these civilisations in turn, from the Chavin to the Inca. It also examines what happened to the Inca Empire and its people after 1532 when the Spanish *conquistador*, Francisco Pizarro, and a small band of men arrived in the area looking for gold and other treasures.

HOW DO WE KNOW?

Most of our knowledge of Peru before 1535 comes from archaeological evidence, as none of the civilisations before that date had a system of writing. Even the archaeological evidence is not as rich as might be

INTRODUCTION

expected from civilisations which were flourishing as recently as 1530. This is because the Spanish *conquistadors* ransacked and destroyed many Inca towns and villages, seizing gold and silver objects to be melted down for bullion. They also destroyed any evidence of the Inca religion that they found, as they forced people to become Christians. In more recent times, grave-robbing has become a serious problem, as newly discovered graves are stripped of any treasure or other valuable artefacts. In spite of this, some remains have survived remarkably well. They include the ruins of the town of Machu Picchu, the tombs at Sipan, and the mysterious lines and pictures in the Nazca desert, all of which have been rediscovered in the 20th century. Scientific analysis of some of the surviving mummified bodies has revealed clues about what people died from, the diseases they suffered and even something of what they ate and drank immediately before death.

There are also accounts of Inca life and customs written by Spanish priests and soldiers in the years immediately after the conquest, and a collection of drawings of the Incas made in the early 17th century by Poma de Ayala, who had an Inca mother and a Spanish father. However, these accounts and illustrations may not be entirely accurate, partly because they relied on other people's memories of what happened in the past, and partly because the Spaniards wrote from a European viewpoint which saw the Incas as backward and inferior to themselves.

Among Poma de Ayala's drawings of the Incas are some that illustrate the farming year. This one represents March and shows the guardian of the maize field scaring away birds with a sling-shot and a stick hung with bells.

FROM THE FIRST PEOPLE TO THE CHAVIN

The first people arrived in Peru between 12,000 and 10,000 years ago. They lived by hunting and gathering food from the wild, living in temporary shelters as they moved around in search of edible plants and animals. Two thousand years later, they were making their first attempts at cultivating some wild plants, including grasses, beans, peppers and squash in the fertile valleys, but they still made their homes in temporary dwellings. By 6000 BC some grasses were being grown at higher altitudes, where potatoes were also being cultivated from the wild. It was only after about 3000 BC, however, that the cultivation of plants was successful enough to allow people to settle permanently for longer periods in one place. Their earliest dwellings were conical-shaped huts, made from a framework of poles stuck into the ground in a circle, tied together at the top and thatched with grass or reeds.

Like many of the rivers in Peru, the Ocona River flows west from the Andes Mountains to the coast. People in the river valleys along the coast were able to channel water to irrigate their fields.

THE FIRST SETTLEMENTS

Once people had a more reliable source of food, the population expanded and the first villages and towns began to develop. Between 4000 and 5000 years ago villages appeared on the coast where fish,

FROM THE FIRST PEOPLE TO THE CHAVIN

shellfish and other sea creatures formed the daily diet. Around the same time, people also began to settle in the valleys of the rivers that crossed the desert between the mountains and the coast. There was very little rainfall in this area. However, the rivers flowed all year round as they were fed by streams in the mountains where rain was plentiful. Using this knowledge, the settlers developed simple irrigation systems which allowed them to grow the plants they had cultivated. They added to their diet by domesticating ducks for their meat and hunting wild fowl and catching fish from the rivers.

Around the same time, people were also beginning to settle down in the highlands. The main food crop was potatoes, while protein came from guinea pigs which were domesticated and eaten. However, the most important animals in the highlands were four different breeds of camelids (animals which are related to camels). These were the vicuña, the guanaco, the llama and the alpaca, all of which grazed on the large areas of *puna* between the mountain ranges. At first, all these animals were hunted for their meat, but by 2500 BC both llamas and alpacas had been domesticated, though the vicuña and the guanaco remained untamed.

Llamas still graze in the Andes today. These animals are in a pasture at around 4000 metres above sea level.

A CLOSER LOOK

Llamas and alpacas were very important to the farmers of Peru. Both animals provided meat and hides, as well as dung which could be dried and burned as fuel. They also provided wool. Llama wool was harsh and strong and could be spun and used for ropes, blankets and other heavy cloth. Alpaca wool was very fine and was woven to make warm clothing. Once they had been tamed, llamas were also used as transport, carrying loads on their backs over the steep and narrow paths through the mountains. Some were also used in religious rituals and ceremonies (see page 42).

A gold model of a llama. It was made by the Incas as an offering to their gods.

TOWARDS CIVILISATIONS

A settled lifestyle and more reliable sources of food allowed an increasingly organised society to develop, and by about 2300 BC people began to construct large-scale building projects. One of the earliest to be discovered so far is at Aspero, on the coast to the north of Lima, where, over several centuries, six rectangular platforms were built. These platforms rose up to a height of ten metres and were topped with stone buildings, used for burials and religious purposes. Another temple, in the highlands of the Andes at La Galgada, was used for burials and for agricultural ceremonies. It was built of stone and mud around 2300 BC and its walls were plastered and painted. The tombs inside the temple contained the bodies of the local nobility, while ordinary people were buried outside the walls, suggesting that society was already forming into several, distinct social classes.

From items left in these and other temples and tombs, we know that people in these settlements traded goods over a large area. They obtained cotton and coloured shells from the people on the coast, and wool and root crops from people in the highlands. They traded for coloured feathers and hallucinogenic snuffs from the people in the rainforests to the east of the Andes. By 2000 BC they had added maize to the list of crops they cultivated. They had also begun to make pottery vessels to replace the plant gourds previously used for both storing and cooking food.

From around 1700 BC, people began to build much larger ceremonial centres. These were also on mounds and usually had a U-shaped temple as their most important structure. Their size suggests that they were built by people from more than one village which, in turn, suggests that a new sort of society was beginning to develop, paving the way for the first complex civilisation.

This pottery jar from the Moche civilisation (see pages 20-22) shows a woman wearing a headdress made from maize cobs. She is possibly a goddess.

THE CHAVIN CIVILISATION

The first well-developed civilisation in Peru was the Chavin. Its name is taken from a site called Chavin de Huantar, a temple complex which flourished 3200 metres up in the northern highlands of Peru between about 850 and 200 BC. The Chavin culture began to develop around 900 BC and, at its height around 500 BC, its influence spread throughout most of northern and central Peru and along much of the south coast. Nobody knows for certain, but it seems unlikely that all these places were united

A CLOSER LOOK

Some of what we consider to be dangerous drugs today were widely used by the Incas and their predecessors. Priests and shamans often took hallucinogenic snuff to help them in their religious ceremonies and to predict the future. Many other people chewed the leaves of the coca plant as part of their everyday lives. It is thought that this helped them to cope with the problems of tiredness and hunger which are a result of living at a high altitude.

People still chew coca leaves in Peru today.

politically under one ruler. Instead they were linked by their religion, which archaeologists have learned much about from the remains at Chavin de Huantar.

THE TEMPLE COMPLEX

Chavin de Huantar stands on one of the few passes through the Andes that remains snow-free all year. The oldest part of its temple complex is a U-shaped structure, with its open end facing east. It is built on top of platforms of stone rubble, faced with smooth stone. Inside these platforms are several rooms and galleries, including one containing pottery vessels which were brought from different parts of Peru to Chavin de Huantar, suggesting that it was a place of pilgrimage. Most of the vessels at the site were broken, but the bones of guinea pigs, fish, llamas and deer found amongst the pieces of pottery suggest that they once contained food offerings.

Many of the images found in and around the temple at Chavin de Huantar have fierce, snarling faces. This one also carries severed heads on its belt, as trophies of victories over its enemies.

IMAGES OF THE GODS

The temple complex at Chavin de Huantar was built of huge blocks of stone, including white granite and black andesite, on which there are carved images of many different gods. Archaeologists believe that three of these images were more important than the others, either because their images are bigger or because they have also been found in later civilisations. No one knows their original names, but archaeologists have called the first one the Great Image, the Smiling God or El Lanzón, meaning 'the lance'. It has long fangs, a snarling expression and

FROM THE FIRST PEOPLE TO THE CHAVIN

A CLOSER LOOK
Many of the Chavin temples contained oracles through which the gods 'spoke' to the people. It is thought that the effect was achieved by a hidden priest talking through a trumpet made from a conch shell. These shells were found on the coast of Ecuador and were traded along the length of the Andes.

hair like snakes, and is carved into a narrow piece of rock which is four and a half metres tall. The second is the Staff God which has a human body but a feline face and holds a staff in either hand (see page 38). Both of these are in the temple, but the third one is in a courtyard and is the image of a cayman carved into an oblong pillar. Other carvings on the walls at Chavin include jaguars, eagles, snakes and parrots and these, together with images of the Staff God, continue to appear in various forms on stone carvings, pottery, textiles, and gold and silver objects through to Inca times.

A twin-handled pot, known as a stirrup pot, made in Chavin de Huantar. It is decorated with the image of the Smiling God.

EVERYDAY LIFE

Archaeologists believe that Chavin de Huantar grew from a settlement of around 500 farmers and herders in 850 BC to a town of around 2000 to 3000 people by 250 BC. Its most important inhabitants lived in tall, stone houses, built on wide terraces surrounding the temple complex, and separate from the rest of the population. They ate meat from young llamas and wore jewellery, including rings, ear-discs and pendants made from gold. Most other towns of the period grew up separately from the temple complexes. As well as farmers, herders and traders, the inhabitants included people who were not directly involved in the production of food, such as goldsmiths, silversmiths, potters, stone-carvers and textile workers.

THE PARACAS, NAZCA AND MOCHE

During the third century BC the Chavin civilisation began to collapse, but with no written records, no one today can be sure why this happened. One possibility is that the various communities began to develop in different ways and, without the firm structure of a state to hold them together, they gradually drifted apart. The ceremonial centres were abandoned and at Chavin de Huantar farmers used some of the carved stones from the temple to build the walls of their houses. Several centuries would pass before another distinct civilisation developed in the highlands, but in this same period archaeologists have identified various civilisations on the coast and in the short river valleys that cross the desert.

THE PARACAS CIVILISATION

The oldest civilisation on the coast of Peru is that of the Paracas which probably began to develop before 600 BC, when the Chavin was still flourishing, and lasted until about AD 175. One of the most extraordinary sites of the Paracas civilisation was the windswept, treeless Paracas peninsula which juts out into the Pacific Ocean between the valleys of the Pisco and Ica rivers. This peninsula seems to have been a ritual centre, and a number of cemeteries complete with mummified bodies have been discovered there. However, the people of the Paracas civilisation lived north of this peninsula, in river valleys near the coast. Much of the information about

A CLOSER LOOK
The name Paracas comes from a Quechuan word which means 'sand falling like rain' and is used to describe the sandstorms that start abruptly on the peninsula towards the end of each afternoon and die away equally abruptly at dusk.

the Paracas civilisation has come from archaeological excavations. The dry climate of this area has helped to preserve the remains of food and artefacts such as textiles and featherwork which would have rotted away in damper places. The excavation of various settlement sites has showed that the Paracas people ate maize, peanuts and cassava and got most of their protein from fish. They also made baskets and used plant gourds for containers. However, the cemeteries were even more revealing, as the bodies buried in them were not only mummified but also wrapped up in bundles of cloth, most of which contained grave goods of various kinds.

A mummy bundle from one of the cemeteries on the Paracas peninsula. Underneath all the wrappings the bodies were naked and mummified naturally in the hot sand.

Unlike Ancient Egyptian mummies which had their limbs straightened out, Paracas mummies were usually in a sitting position with their knees tucked up towards their chins. They were enclosed in a piece of plain, cotton cloth. Ordinary people were buried like this, but more important people were placed inside a large, shallow basket which was then wrapped around with more layers of cloth until it made a large, cone-shaped bundle. Some of the layers of cloth were plain, but others were richly patterned with panels of embroidery, showing images of plants and animals, humans, gods and mythical creatures, some of which were similar to those used by the Chavin people.

Many of the bundles contained intricately woven and embroidered clothing such as skirts and tunics, mantles, loincloths and *ruanas* (ponchos), as well as headbands made from fur and feathers. Some also had simple gold ornaments tucked between the layers of cloth or in the mouth of the mummy, and some were surrounded by pottery objects, especially bowls and bottles with double spouts joined by a handle. It seems likely that the embroidery on the burial cloths related to the person's status in life, but not enough is known about the Paracas religion to decide whether the other objects were meant to be used in another life, or were given as gifts for the gods.

This pottery figure of a seated woman is from the Nazca civilisation. The lump on her cheek represents a wad of coca leaves, but no one is certain whether the marks under her eyes are spots or tattoos.

THE NAZCA CIVILISATION

Around the time that the Chavin civilisation was collapsing, another new civilisation was developing in the river valleys on the southern coast of Peru. Named Nazca after the valley on which it was centred, its influence spread north and south to include the Pisco, Chincha, Ica, Palpo and Acari valleys. Its people lived mainly by farming, developing underground irrigation channels, called *pukios*, to make it possible to grow large crops of maize, beans and peppers in the harsh, desert climate. Their textiles and pottery shared similarities with those of the nearby Paracas people. Later they developed their own distinctive styles, especially in pottery where four or more colours were often used in painted designs featuring people, plants, birds, fish and animals. Some were realistic, but others were mythical creatures and demons with elongated features. Towards the end of the Nazca period images of trophy heads (heads that were cut from the bodies of defeated enemies and taken as trophies or prizes) were used in designs on both textiles and pottery. Mummified human heads, probably from prisoners taken in combat, have also been found at some Nazca sites. It is thought that these heads were used in religious ceremonies to ensure good harvests.

The main centre of the Nazca religion was at Cahuachi in the Nazca valley where platform mounds and huge adobe pyramids, separated by courts and plazas, were built over a period of about 700 years. The largest construction is the Great Temple which is a stepped pyramid almost 20 metres high. Thousands of people were buried in cemeteries surrounding Cahuachi. Like the Paracas people, they were placed in a sitting position, wrapped in cloth and given grave goods which included pottery and ornaments made from hammered gold.

However, the most spectacular and puzzling remains of the Nazca civilisation are the so-called Nazca Lines on the surface of the desert next to the Nazca valley. These include straight lines and geometric shapes, as well as enormous drawings of

The spider was the first figure to be recognised by María Reiche (see page 20) when she began studying the Nazca Lines in 1946. Like the rest of the lines, it survived through the centuries because the extreme dryness of the area prevented plants and grasses growing over it.

A CLOSER LOOK
After the collapse of the Nazca civilisation, in the 8th century AD, the Nazca Lines went unnoticed until the 1920s, when they were thought to be ancient roads crossing the desert. Their true significance was not rediscovered until the 1940s when the German archaeologist, María Reiche, began to examine them. She studied them over many decades and eventually concluded that they were used for astronomical purposes.

plants and animals. They were made by removing the small stones that cover the surface of the desert to reveal the light-coloured soil underneath. The animals represented by the lines include a monkey, a killer whale, a spider and a hummingbird, while the geometric shapes include triangles and trapezoids. There are many different theories as to why they were created. Some people think they tie in with solar or astronomical observations, while others think they point to sacred places in the mountains or relate to the irrigation systems. Another theory is that they were offerings to the gods, made in times of extreme drought or other disasters. They might also have been created as pathways for religious processions, as some of the designs are made up of a single line which makes it possible to walk all the way around without retracing your steps.

THE MOCHE CIVILISATION

While the Paracas and Nazca civilisations flourished in the coastal region of southern Peru, the Moche (or Mochica) civilisation developed on the northern coast. Starting around AD 1, it lasted to around AD 800. Its name is taken from the site of Moche in the valley of the Moche River, from where its influence spread for over 350 kilometres between the Lambayeque valley in the north and the Nepena valley in the south.

Like the Paracas and Nazca people, the Moche built an extensive irrigation system which enabled them to grow large crops of maize, beans, peppers, peanuts and sweet potatoes in the rainless valleys. They also built urban centres, the most important of which was Moche itself, near the present-day town of

THE PARACAS, NAZCA AND MOCHE

Trujillo. The settlement there is dominated by two huge structures, known as the Pyramid of the Sun and the Pyramid of the Moon, surrounded by evidence of a densely populated city.

The two large pyramids at Moche were religious and ceremonial centres, but many other pyramids in the region were the tombs of an elite class of warrior-priests. Most of them have been robbed over the centuries, but in 1987 archaeologists were able to excavate one which was almost intact at Huaca Rajada, near Sipan in the Lambayeque valley. An outer tomb in the pyramid had been ransacked by grave-robbers, but an inner tomb contained an undisturbed wooden coffin with gold and feather headdresses, clothing decorated with gold, silver and copper, banners, shell beads, and gold and silver jewellery decorated with precious stones. They also found the body of a man who had been about 40 years old

A reconstruction of the Royal Tomb at Sipan. The man known as the Lord of Sipan was buried in the large coffin in the centre.

when he died in around AD 300. Nicknamed the Lord of Sipan, he was buried with two men and three women, all in separate coffins, plus a third man who had been buried without a coffin and with his feet cut off, probably to prevent him running away. As well as its beautiful artefacts, this discovery has added to archaeologists' knowledge of the Moche civilisation by showing that its influence extended far beyond the Moche Valley, while the number and status of the people in the tomb are further evidence of the complexity of Moche society.

Apart from the tomb of the Lord of Sipan, the Moche civilisation is probably most famous for its pottery. Many Moche vessels were painted with scenes from everyday life or with scenes of religious or political rituals. Others were modelled into the shape of people or animals and depict many aspects of everyday life, while some jars are in the shape of human faces, often with such realistic features that they must almost certainly have been portraits of actual people. Many pots also show warriors and aspects of the warfare which probably helped the Moche civilisation to expand as far as it did.

Despite its wealth, the Moche civilisation collapsed around AD 800. There are several possibly reasons: a succession of natural disasters such as earthquakes, prolonged drought, sand dunes drifting on to populated areas, or even flooding caused by the climatic condition known as El Niño.

This stirrup pot is in the shape of a Moche chief. It was filled or emptied through the spout which is in the middle of the looped, hollow handle behind the head.

THE TIAHUANACO, HUARI AND CHIMU

Lake Titicaca lies high in the Andes Mountains. Today, the Uru people continue to make boats from bundles of dried totora reeds, just as the people of Tiahuanaco did over 1500 years ago.

Following the collapse of the Chavin, there was no unifying civilisation in the highlands for several centuries. People carried on farming and trading, making textiles and pottery, but they lived in individual communities with very little influence beyond their own immediate area. Eventually, however, some communities in the highlands around Lake Titicaca in what is now Bolivia became more powerful and developed into small city-states, of which the best-known are Pucara and Chiripa. The area of influence of these city-states was limited, but they were followed by others which became powerful enough to start the unification of the peoples of the highlands once more. The first civilisation to develop in this way was Tiahuanaco near the southern shore of Lake Titicaca.

THE TIAHUANACO CIVILISATION

People began to settle in the area of Tiahuanaco around 1000 BC, but construction of the temple complex, the ruins of which can be seen today, was probably started around the first century AD. The civilisation itself did not begin to expand until around AD 500.

At an altitude of 3660 metres above sea level, Tiahuanaco was the highest ancient city in the Andes. It was also in one of the bleakest landscapes. Situated on the *altiplano*, the treeless *puna* provides

The huge Ponce monolith at Tiahunanaco represents one of the many gods worshipped there.

no shelter from the biting winds. In spite of this, its farmers were able to grow enough food to feed a population which numbered possibly as many as 50,000 people at its height. They did this by means of the raised-field system which reclaimed land from the marshy areas near the shore of the lake. Crops were planted in specially prepared platforms measuring between four and nine metres wide and between nine and 90 metres long. The platforms stood about one metre above the surrounding area and the extra soil needed to make them was obtained by digging out channels around them. The channels were then filled with water which absorbed the heat of the sun during the day and released it at night as the air temperature fell sharply. This protected the plants from frost damage and also extended the growing season, while the algae and water plants that flourished in the canals were dug out and used as fertilisers on the fields. These measures made it possible to produce two crops each year.

The abundance of food produced by the raised-field system meant that not everybody had to work on the land in order to eat. In turn, this allowed Tiahuanaco to develop into a ceremonial and religious centre with many fine structures made from massive stone blocks that were imported from across Lake Titicaca. These structures include the Akapana Pyramid, a stepped platform made from earth and faced with cut stone which had several temples on the top, a partially underground temple with stone heads fixed into the walls, and a low, oblong platform called the Kalassasaya. In one corner of the Kalassasaya there

A CLOSER LOOK

Archaeologists believe that the influence of the civilisation of Tiahuanaco spread through trade and a shared religion, rather than through warfare and conquest, as no evidence of fortifications or weapons has been found. They think that the city of Tiahuanaco was a centre of pilgrimage. People travelled great distances to the city to see the stone carvings, some of which were on pillars up to seven metres in height.

is a huge doorway, sometimes called the Gateway of the Sun, which is cut from a single block of basalt, a type of volcanic rock. A figure carved over the centre of the doorway looks very like the Staff God of the Chavin civilisation, and is flanked on either side by three rows of carved, winged figures. Archaeologists have nicknamed this figure the Gateway God, and his image and that of the winged figures are found on stone carvings and pottery throughout the whole area influenced by Tiahuanaco.

The civilisation of Tiahuanaco reached its greatest extent between about AD 500 and 1000. During this time its influence covered large parts of what are now south and east Bolivia, southern Peru, northern

The Gateway of the Sun is one of the few ancient structures to have survived at Tiahuanaco.

This map shows the main places mentioned in Chapters Three and Four.

Quito
Chan Chan · Sipan
· Cajamarca
Moche · La Galgada
· Chavin de Huantar
Aspero ·
Lima
Paracas ·
· Huari
· Cuzco
Nazca · Pikillacta
Pacific Ocean
Lake Titicaca
Key
■ Present-day cities
Tiahuanaco
0 — 200 miles
0 — 200 km

Chile and the northwest of Argentina. But despite this success, Tiahuanaco declined in the 10th century AD, possibly as the result of a prolonged drought which made it impossible to grow enough food to feed its people. Its inhabitants dispersed throughout the mountains and valleys of the southern Andes.

THE HUARI CIVILISATION

The Huari civilisation began to develop around AD 600 in the central highlands of Peru. It is named after the town of Huari on which it was centred. Its people cut terraces in the steep hillsides to make flat areas on which they could grow crops (you can read more about this on page 43). Apart from this, it had much in common with Tiahuanaco, including the images of the Gateway God and his attendants which are found on Huari textiles, pottery, stone carvings and artefacts in gold and copper. However, no one knows exactly how, or even if, the two civilisations were connected to each other.

A CLOSER LOOK

The Huari built administrative centres throughout their empire. One of these was at Pikillacta, around 30 kilometres from where the Incas would later build their capital, Cuzco. Pikillacta was built to a square grid pattern and contained over 700 buildings, some of which were three storeys high. The walls of the buildings were of rough stone, set in a cement made from mud and plastered over with coats of clay to make them smooth. This was in contrast to the buildings at Tiahuanaco which were constructed from massive stone blocks, cut and shaped so carefully that no mortar was needed to hold them together.

THE TIAHUANACO, HUARI AND CHIMU

By AD 800 the Huari sphere of influence stretched north as far as the Cajamara and Chicama valleys and south as far as the Ocona valley. It seems to have been run as an empire, with palaces and rich tombs in Huari suggesting there was a distinct ruling class, and large-scale storage facilities and evidence of record-keeping in the town suggesting that some sort of tribute was paid as taxes. However, there are conflicting views about how its influence spread. Some people believe that the empire expanded through military conquest, but others think that its expansion was through trade and the spread of a shared religion. The Huari empire reached its greatest extent around AD 800, then for some unknown reason people began to abandon the city of Huari and the civilisation started to collapse. By around AD 900 Huari itself had been abandoned and many people in the highlands had gone back to living in small rural communities rather than in large urban centres.

The skills of Chimu goldsmiths can be seen in this figure which is part of the hilt of a ceremonial knife, or tumi.

THE CHIMU CIVILISATION

Following the collapse of the Huari and Tiahuanaco civilisations, Peru was once more divided up into small, independent states, most of which were confined to their own river valleys. One of these states was that of the Chimu in the Moche valley on the north coast of Peru. The Chimu inhabited this valley by about AD 1000, although initial settlement was probably as early as AD 800. Like all the people before them, they irrigated the dry land and grew maize and other crops to feed themselves. They were skilled at weaving, featherwork and making pottery. Chimu metalworkers also

A CLOSER LOOK

Today, the ruins of Chan Chan cover an area of around 25 square kilometres. They are in a good state of preservation because so little rain falls in the area. The city is divided into rectangular blocks of buildings separated by streets. At its centre there are about ten large enclosures, known as *ciudadelas*, surrounded by adobe and rammed earth walls which are about three metres wide at their base and about nine metres high. It is thought that these citadels were palaces and that a new one was built for each successive ruler, while the old ones were sealed up. Each *ciudadela* had just one door leading from the outside into a large courtyard. Beyond this was a complex of storerooms and courtyards, probably used for storing and distributing goods which had been obtained as tax or tribute. The royal living quarters were along one side of the *ciudadela* and, after death, the ruler was buried within the *ciudadela* with his worldly possessions.

Details of a frieze at Chan Chan (right) and the ruins of one of the ciudadelas *(below)*

produced magnificent artefacts in gold, silver and copper which were often decorated with a mosaic pattern of semi-precious stones such as turquoise. Around AD 1200 the Chimu started to build their capital city, Chan Chan (see box). Early in the following century, as the size of their population increased, they began to expand the territory under their control by means of conquest.

The Chimu Empire and society

By 1450 the Chimu controlled an empire which stretched along the coast from Piura in the north almost to present-day Lima in the south. The empire was run from Chan Chan and roads were constructed to make trade and communications easier. Cities were also built in other parts of the empire. These cities were similar in layout to Chan Chan and probably served as local centres of administration, where taxes and tribute could be collected and distributed. Society was divided into distinct classes, with peasants and farmers at the bottom and a powerful aristocracy at the top, led by a ruler who was probably thought to be a god. In the middle were craftworkers, many of whom were highly respected.

The decline of the Chimu

Although Chimu was a powerful and well-organised state, it was conquered by the Incas in 1476. One possible reason for this is that it depended on its irrigation systems to feed its population. If these failed, people went hungry. Oral tradition says that the Incas realised this and stopped the supply of water to the canals around Chan Chan. However, another tradition says that the Chimu decided that the Incas' weapons were too powerful for them to resist. Another possibility is that the cost of maintaining all the disused palaces in Chan Chan (see box) used up wealth which should have gone into strengthening the empire, and this made it easier for the Incas to gain control and make the Chimu lands part of their own empire.

THE RISE OF THE INCAS

The last widespread civilisation to develop in Peru before 1535 was that of the Incas. According to tradition, the rise of the Incas started towards the end of the 12th century AD. At this time the highlands of Peru were once more divided up into many different communities, following the collapse of the Tiahuanaco and Huari civilisations. Like all the earlier civilisations in South America the Incas had no written language, so the story of their origins was passed down by word of mouth from one generation to the next. It was eventually written down by the Spaniards, but by that time nobody knew for certain what was fact and what was myth.

INCA ORIGINS

Inca tradition says that the Inca civilisation started around AD 1200, when Manco Capac decided to move his people about 25 kilometres north from the village of

A CLOSER LOOK

Although the Incas had no system of writing, specially trained government officials kept records on lengths of knotted string, known as *quipus* (left). The position and size of a knot related to the number it represented. For example, a simple knot represented one, while longer knots stood for numbers up to nine. A knot with three loops at the bottom of the string was three, but if it was further up it represented 30. Further up still it was 300 and at the top of the string it was 3000 or 30,000. Different coloured strings related to different items that were being counted.

THE RISE OF THE INCAS

Paqaritampu to the site of present-day Cuzco. Today, no one knows whether Manco Capac was a real or a legendary leader, or why he decided to move his people when he did. He might have been looking for better farming land: one legend relates that he and his sister, Mama Huaca, took with them a magic, golden rod which had been given to them by Inti, the Sun god. Inti told them to settle at the place where they could push the rod deep into the ground, because the soil would be good and fertile for growing crops. They kept trying and finally succeeded at the place which became their capital, Cuzco.

TOWARDS AN EMPIRE

The Emperor Pachacuti, as drawn by Poma de Ayala in about 1620

During the 200 years after they settled in Cuzco, the Incas gradually grew more powerful. They attacked and defeated neighbouring communities in the Cuzco valley, but they did not attempt to take control of them. Instead, the Incas forced the defeated peoples to pay tribute (tax) in exchange for their freedom. In the 14th century, the Incas made their first conquests of lands outside the Cuzco valley. Again this was only on a small scale and no Inca officials were sent to rule over the defeated peoples. Then in 1438 a new ruler came to the Inca throne. His name was Pachacuti Inca Yupanqui and he claimed to be a direct descendant of the gods of Tihuanaco. As well as being ambitious, he was also a military genius. He set out to conquer the neighbouring lands by force and make them all part of an Inca Empire.

CHAPTER FIVE

A TIME OF RAPID EXPANSION

In less than 100 years from the start of Pachacuti's rule, the Incas expanded the territory under their control until they had an empire which stretched for over 3500 kilometres from north to south and an average of 320 kilometres from east to west. The empire had a population of between ten and twelve million people. This expansion was achieved by the determination of just three rulers. Between 1438 and 1463 Pachacuti and his army conquered the central highlands to the west of Cuzco. He then turned his attention to ruling his expanding empire and handed the task of further conquest on to his son, Topa Inca.

While Pachacuti was still alive, Topa Inca conquered the Chimu lands. He also tried to invade the Amazonian rainforest, but was unsuccessful

Cuzco is overlooked by the Inca fortress of Sacsayhuaman. It is said that 20,000 people worked on the construction of this fortress. Some of the stones are over six metres tall and weigh more than 100 tonnes.

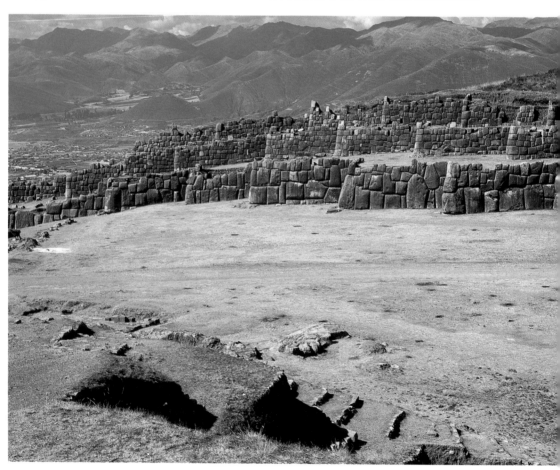

THE RISE OF THE INCAS

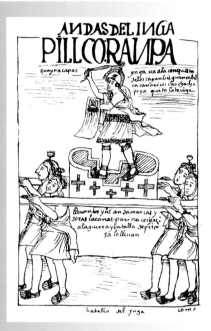

because his army found it difficult to fight amongst the dense vegetation. When he became Sapa Inca (meaning Sole Ruler) in 1471, Topa headed south to conquer the southern highlands and coastal areas. However, when he reached the centre of present-day Chile he met strong resistance from the Araucanian people and, after a fierce battle, he decided to make this the southern boundary of the Inca Empire.

After Topa's death in 1493, his son Huayna Capac became the next Sapa Inca. He added parts of the northern highlands and coastal areas as far as present-day Quito to the empire. But before he could go any further he was taken ill and died in 1525.

CONTROLLING THE EMPIRE

As his empire grew ever larger, Pachacuti devised ways of ruling it from his capital, Cuzco. He employed thousands of officials who worked throughout the empire. He also set up a network of roads to give access between Cuzco and the rest of the empire. This network allowed the army to move quickly to any part of the empire. It meant that vital supplies such as food and other goods could be

33

The ruins of Tambo Colorado, one of the resting-places for Inca messengers, can still be seen in the coastal desert of Peru today.

As an Inca messenger approached a hut, he blew into a conch shell horn to alert the next messenger.

transported easily. The roads were vital for communication, too. The emperor sent and received orders and information from all corners of the empire by means of official messengers. These messengers lived in huts which were placed two kilometres apart on every road. They learned each message by heart, then ran with it to the next hut to pass it on. In this way, information could travel up to 250 kilometres in a single day. Pachacuti and later emperors also kept control of the Inca lands by building new towns in the conquered territories and sending teachers to the conquered peoples to show them the Inca way of life. Those who accepted this way of life were usually allowed to remain in their own

THE RISE OF THE INCAS

A CLOSER LOOK
The Incas called their empire Tahuantisuyu, which means 'The Land of the Four Quarters'. This was because the empire was divided into four provinces, or *suyus*, each representing one of the four main points of the compass, with Cuzco at the centre. Each province was further divided into smaller units, made up of a number of *ayllus*, or communities. The Inca rulers made everyone wear the distinctive clothing of their village or *ayllu*, so that they were easily identifiable.

communities, but groups from problematic communities were sometimes moved to distant parts of the empire. They were replaced in the community by groups of more loyal people who would report any misdeeds to the Inca rulers. This policy was intended to discourage any large-scale rebellion against the Incas.

TAXES

The Incas kept their empire running by taxing people in two different ways. Each community used about one third of its land to grow crops for the Inca, and another third to grow crops for the gods, while the rest was used to grow crops for themselves. People also produced a certain amount of textiles for the Inca each year. On top of this there was a labour tax, known as *mit'a*, which all able-bodied men between the ages of about 16 and 60 had to pay by working for the empire for a certain period each year. This work included serving in the army, building roads, working on irrigation and drainage schemes, constructing terraces for agriculture, quarrying stone, mining gold and helping to build new towns and fortresses. In return, the Inca rulers made sure that everyone was fed and clothed, even in times of poor harvests, and many of the crops dedicated to the gods were returned to the people during religious feasts and ceremonies.

A CLOSER LOOK
Quipus (see page 30) were used to keep a record of the goods provided by each *ayllu* for the Sapa Inca, the number of people living in each household, and how many households there were in each *ayllu*. Unfortunately, most of the *quipus* were destroyed by the Spaniards who thought they were the work of the devil, and the skill of using them was lost. Some still survive, but none of them can be understood today.

INCA SOCIETY AND EVERYDAY LIFE

Legend says that the first Incas were Manco Capac, his three brothers and four sisters. They emerged from the middle cave of three at Paqaritampu. Manco Capac married Mama Huaca, who was one of his sisters, and they had a son. This son, Sinchi Roca, became Sapa Inca when Manco Capac died. After that, although the Sapa Inca was allowed to have many wives, at least one of them had to be his sister, known as the Coya, to provide an heir. Like the Sapa Inca himself, the Coya was thought to be a child of the Sun. By marrying her, the Sapa Inca ensured that his heir would also be descended directly from the Sun.

This featherwork fan was used by one of the Sapa Inca's slaves to flick the flies from the ruler's face.

The success of the Incas depended on two main factors. The first was their ability to adopt and adapt some of the best features of the earlier civilisations in Peru. The second was their skill at organising their society in such a way that everyone knew their place in it and what was expected of them.

THE SOCIAL STRUCTURE

Inca society was like an enormous pyramid with the Sapa Inca at the top and nobles, who were mainly his relatives, just below him. At first, only these nobles were permitted to help the Sapa Inca with the process of government. But as the empire expanded there were not enough Inca nobles to administer every part. So the Sapa Inca granted privileges to groups close, and loyal, to Cuzco. Later, the Incas allowed cooperative chiefs of conquered lands to continue governing their own territories. These chiefs and their families made up a new class of people, known as the *curacas*. Like the Inca nobles, they did not have to pay any taxes.

INCA SOCIETY AND EVERYDAY LIFE

The long earlobes on this Inca figure show that he was one of the Inca nobility. Nobles were the only group of people allowed to wear very large ear-discs.

To make absolutely certain that these chiefs stayed loyal to the Sapa Inca, their sons were taken to Cuzco as hostages, where they learned how to live and rule according to Inca ways.

Below the *curacas* was a group of less important officials, known as the *camayoq*. Each one was responsible for a certain number of peasant households. Finally, at the bottom of the pyramid came the millions of peasants. They grew the food and paid the taxes that kept the vast Inca Empire running. The whole Inca community was divided up into communities, called *ayllus* (see page 35). Members of an *ayllu* shared common ancestors and worshipped at the same *huacas* (see pages 39-40).

RELIGION

The Incas believed that the world was made by Viracocha, the Creator God. He rose from the waters of Lake Titicaca and lived in Tiahuanaco where he created humans and taught them how to be civilised. He was also the father of the Sun and the Moon and was usually depicted as an old man with a beard. The Staff God at Chavin de Huantar and the Gateway God at Tiahuanaco (see pages 15 and 25) are probably earlier versions of Viracocha.

A CLOSER LOOK

Like the Chimu before them, the Incas preserved the bodies of their rulers and allowed them to carry on 'living' in their palaces after they died. The dead Sapa Inca sat on a golden stool and was served with food every day. A woman stood close by him to whisk away any flies that landed on his face, but most of his personal servants were ceremonially strangled when the Sapa Inca died, so that they could continue to look after him in the afterlife. The palace and all his possessions still belonged to him after death, and all his male descendants, apart from the next Sapa Inca, became his courtiers. The dead Sapa Incas were paraded through the streets of Cuzco on litters during a ceremony known as the Festival of the Dead (right).

CHAPTER SIX

This stone carving of the god Viracocha is from Tiahuanaco. Also known as the Staff God, he would originally have held a staff in each hand.

Viracocha was invisible, but all the other Inca gods and goddesses could be seen or felt and were closely linked to looking after the land, the crops and the animals upon which the people of the Inca Empire depended. The most important was Inti, the Sun god, from whom the Sapa Inca claimed to be descended. Like the Sapa Inca, he was married to his sister, Mama Quilla, who was the Moon goddess. The Inca people also worshipped Pacha Mama who was the Earth goddess, Illapa the god of thunder, rain and war, and Mama Cocha the goddess of the sea who gave the Incas their fish.

INCA TEMPLES

There were temples of various sizes scattered throughout the lands of the Inca Empire. The most important was Coricancha, the temple of the Sun god in the centre of Cuzco. Its walls were covered inside and out with sheets of beaten gold which was the symbol of Inti and was often known as 'the sweat of the Sun'. Inside the walls surrounding the temple was a garden containing models of maize plants and llamas, made from gold and silver. Beyond the garden was a courtyard surrounded by six buildings, each dedicated to a different god. They were also decorated with gold and silver. Inti himself was represented by a huge disc of solid gold at the eastern end of the courtyard. The mummified bodies of the dead Sapa Incas were brought to visit him during important ceremonies.

PRIESTS AND THEIR HELPERS

The most important priest in the Inca religion was the High Priest. He lived in Cuzco and was usually a brother of the Sapa Inca. The priests who helped him were Inca nobles and, although they led a simple, religious life, they were very powerful and had great influence at court. Beneath them came thousands of other priests who lived and worked in temples throughout the empire. They were responsible for organising worship, ceremonies and sacrifices. They also acted as doctors and soothsayers. They were helped in their work by other priests, Handmaidens of the Sun (see box) and servants.

A silver model of a maize plant, similar to those in the garden at Coricancha

HUACAS AND SACRIFICES

As well as temples, there were many places, known as *huacas*, where people could pray and make sacrifices as other Andean peoples had done before

A CLOSER LOOK

When Inca girls were ten years old, they were divided into two groups. The most beautiful ones were sent to *mamacona* institutes, which were rather like convents, to be trained as Chosen Women or *aqlla*. The rest remained in their villages and spent the next two years preparing for marriage. In a *mamacona* institute girls learned about the rituals of Inti worship, as well as how to cook and how to weave vicuña wool into finest cloth for the Sapa Inca and his Coya. After this training, the girls were split up again. Some became wives of high officials or even of the Sapa Inca himself, while a few were sacrificed to the gods. Most became Handmaidens of the Sun and were sent to help the priests in the temples. As well as assisting in ceremonies, they also prepared special food and drink for festivals.

This mamacona *figure is made from silver*

Inca children probably played with dolls made from reeds and cotton, like this one. Some of these dolls were left as sacrifices at huacas.

them. *Huacas* were places such as rocks, springs and caves where local ancestor spirits were thought to have become part of the landscape. Each *huaca* was considered to have special powers, and the Incas made offerings to them when they needed help. These offerings varied according to the importance of the *huaca*, the importance of the request and the wealth of the supplicant. The poorest person might offer a few eyelashes or a small amount of beer, while a rich person might leave a gold ornament or a beautiful garment. At the most powerful *huacas*, sacrifices of guinea pigs and llamas were made. In times of war, severe drought or earthquakes people were also sacrificed.

EVERYDAY LIFE FOR THE PEASANTS

Within each *ayllu*, everyone knew what they were expected to do as both men and women were divided into ten categories, according to their age. Most of the work was done by those between 16 and 60 years old, but even children had to start learning useful skills once they reached the age of two, and old

A CLOSER LOOK

In the harsh climate of Peru, people needed to work together in order to survive. Long before the Incas came to power, many people had organised themselves into large family groups, or *ayllus*. The Incas took this idea and used it as a way of arranging their empire. *Ayllus* varied in size, from the smallest farming village to the city of Cuzco itself, but each one looked after its own members and was responsible for farming its own land.

people were also expected to help in the house and in the fields whenever they could. Women were married at the age of 12 and after that their tasks included cooking, spinning, weaving and looking after the children, while men had to pay the public duty tax, or *mit'a*, as well as making sure they grew enough crops to feed their family and pay their taxes to the Sapa Inca and to the Sun God. Houses for most people were built of stone or adobe bricks and had thatched roofs. They were one storey high and had no real furniture. However, what people ate and how they lived depended on where they lived in the empire. Communities on the coast relied on fishing for their main food supply, while people in the river valleys grew maize, squash, tomatoes, peanuts, beans, peppers and cassava, and kept guinea pigs and ducks for their meat. They also grew cotton which was spun and woven into cloth for their clothes. In the colder highlands, quinoa and white and sweet potatoes were the main food crops, while herds of llamas and alpacas occasionally provided meat as well as wool for clothing and blankets. People also grew the coca plant and chewed its leaves to help them work at high altitudes.

Although it was a hard life, the year was broken up by many religious festivals at which there was often dancing – and plenty of maize beer to drink! If people were too old or ill to work, they were looked after by other members of the *ayllu*, while the state provided them with the food and clothing they needed from what had been gathered in as taxes.

A pottery model of village houses. Buildings were often constructed as closely together as possible in order not take up too much valuable farmland.

SCIENCE AND TECHNOLOGY

When the Spaniards arrived in Peru in 1532, they found a country in which horses and wheeled vehicles were unknown and the skill of working with iron was only just beginning to develop. As the horse, the wheel and ironworking had been essential to the growth of civilisations in much of the Old World for almost 2000 years, the Spaniards thought that the Incas were backward and made no attempt to understand the people or the land they lived in. However, wheeled vehicles would have made very little progress on the steep slopes of the Andes, even if there had been horses to pull them, and the Incas and earlier civilisations in Peru already had tools and weapons which were quite adequate for their needs. In addition, the Incas had developed an efficient system of communication, they knew how to construct large buildings that could withstand earthquakes, they had surgeons who could perform brain operations and blood transfusions, and their farmers were skilled at successfully growing crops in the harshest deserts and on steep mountain slopes.

A CLOSER LOOK

To make the rain start again in October, Inca priests sometimes performed a ritual in which special black llamas were starved until they cried with hunger and thirst. The farmers believed that this crying would make Illapa, the rain god, take pity on the animals and send the rains to quench their thirst.

FARMING

All the civilisations of ancient Peru relied on farmers to exploit the many different types of terrain and climate across the region, and grow enough food to sustain the whole population. In the coastal desert, where almost no rain fell, farmers made irrigation channels to channel water to the fields from the rivers which flowed from the

SCIENCE AND TECHNOLOGY

Andes to the sea. With no natural shelter from the heat of the sun or the drying wind, water soon evaporated if it flowed in the open air. To prevent this happening, many of the channels were roofed over with flat stones and covered with soil.

In the mountains there was plenty of rain, but it did not fall all year round so farmers built stone reservoirs to store rainwater. They also made more flat land available for farming by constructing terraces on the steep mountain slopes. This involved building long stone walls along the contour of the mountainside and then bringing soil up from the valley and piling it behind each wall. The soil was

Land terraced for agriculture at Pisac, above the valley of the Vilcanota river

A CLOSER LOOK

High in the Andes the main crop was potatoes of various kinds. After they had been harvested, the potatoes were left outside at night where they quickly froze in the sub-zero temperatures. They were then dried in the hot sun to produce a food called *chunu* which could be stored and eaten when fresh food was scarce. Strips of meat were also preserved in this way for later use.

Much of the gold used by the peoples of ancient Peru came from streams and rivers. It was found as nuggets or tiny specks mixed in with the gravel on the river bed. The gold was heated until it turned to liquid. This required a temperature of almost 2000° C, which the metalworkers achieved by blowing through tubes into a brazier filled with burning charcoal. A clay pot or crucible containing the ore was placed directly into the fire and the molten gold collected at the bottom of it. It was then poured into moulds to form ingots of pure gold before being used to make beautiful ornaments or jewellery.

levelled off to give a flat surface on which to grow crops. To keep the soil fertile, animal and human manure was spread on it, but the best fertiliser was thought to be the droppings of sea birds. During the dry season, which lasted from June to September in the mountains, the terraces were irrigated with water brought in channels from the reservoirs.

TOOLS AND WEAPONS

From before Chavin times, people made both tools and weapons from stone, wood and animal bone. They used a kind of volcanic glass, called obsidian, to make knife blades with a cutting edge as sharp as steel. They shaped other stones into axeheads and hammerheads which could be held in the hand or fixed on to wooden handles. Digging-sticks made from wood were used to turn the soil before planting seeds. For attack and defence, people used heavy wooden clubs, some of which were tipped with stone or bronze for stabbing as well as hitting. Other weapons included wooden lances and spears, and bows and arrows which were used for hunting.

BUILDING TECHNIQUES

In the desert along the coast, people constructed their houses and other buildings from adobe bricks. These buildings lasted well in areas where there was very little rainfall, but they would have soon disintegrated in the heavy rain and snow that fell in the mountains. People in the highlands used stone to construct their buildings. Although they had no iron tools, no explosives and no lifting equipment, they were able to cut and move stones weighing up to 100 tonnes. No one is certain how they did this, but it is thought that stonemasons looked for natural

Some Inca walls still stand today in the former capital of Cuzco.

A paved Inca road near Intipunku in the Andes. The roads were built and maintained by farmers as part of their labour tax.

cracks in the stone in a quarry and then forced wooden wedges into them. The wood was then soaked with water until it expanded and made the crack wider and deeper. This process was repeated until it was possible to free the block of stone with the help of wood or bronze crowbars and stone hammers. Ropes were fastened around the stone and it was dragged to the building site by large teams of men. There it was cut into the required size with stone hammers and axes.

The great skill of Tiahuanacan and Inca building, however, was in the shaping of the stone. Again this was done with stone hammers and possibly also bronze chisels and no two stones were ever quite the same size and shape. The stones had many faces and sometimes as many as 30 corners, but they all interlocked perfectly with each other and no mortar was needed to hold the walls together. This precise fit allowed many of these structures to survive earthquakes with very little damage.

ROADS

Like the Chimu before them, the Incas built a vast system of roads to link all parts of their empire. The two most important roads ran the full length of the empire, one through the mountains and the other across the coastal desert. The roads were used mainly by the emperor's messengers and by people transporting goods. Their construction varied depending upon the terrain, but they were usually paved with stone. A mixture of clay, pebbles and crushed maize leaves was often used to smooth out rough areas. The roads were built in as straight a line as possible, with flights of steps on the steepest slopes.

Rivers were crossed by various kinds of bridges, depending on their width. Small streams and very narrow rivers were crossed by solid bridges made from wooden planks. If a river was wide, slow-flowing and between low banks, it might be bridged by reed boats fastened together and used as a pontoon. Deep valleys were crossed by suspension bridges, made and maintained by workers from the nearest *ayllus* (see box).

A CLOSER LOOK

Suspension bridges were usually made from rope. Each household in the *ayllu* had to make its share from the dry flower stalks of *q'oya* grass. The women spun a length of two-ply rope with their hands until it was about as thick as a finger. The men then stretched these ropes out in bundles and twisted them into six cables, each about 20 centimetres in diameter. Each cable was braided to stop it untwisting. A stone pillar was built at either side of the valley and the first cable was taken across and firmly fixed at each end. Three more were stretched alongside it to make the bottom of the bridge, then the other two were added as handrails. The four bottom cables were tied together to make a flat platform on which planks of wood could be laid for a walkway and the two handrails were lashed to the bottom to hold the bridge together.

This modern suspension bridge over the River Pampas was made in just the same way as the Inca bridges.

SCIENCE AND TECHNOLOGY

MEDICINE

By Inca times, the people of Peru, their doctors and healers had knowledge of many different remedies for injuries and illnesses. The leaves of the coca plant were chewed to ease pain, stop hunger pangs and help people cope with the harsh climate and altitude, while the leaves of the cassava plant were boiled to make a potion which was good for aching joints. A special type of clay was eaten to try and cure gout, and a mineral called jasper was crushed and used to stop bleeding. People also used quinine as a cure for fevers and to heal wounds. Many of these medicines were obtained from official chemists, known as *hampi camayoc*. Some were also obtained from people called *collahuaya*, who were medical specialists or shamans. They also supplied amulets and lucky charms to ward off illnesses.

This Moche priest is trying to heal the woman laid out in front of him. His eyes are closed as if in concentration, or he may be in a trance.

In the *ayllus*, Inca priests often acted as surgeons. They anaesthetised their patients with coca leaves or *chicha* (beer) and operated on them with knives made from gold, silver, copper, obsidian or flint. They knew how to amputate crushed limbs, set broken bones, pull out teeth and even give blood transfusions.

A CLOSER LOOK

Archaeologists in Peru have found many skulls which have been carefully cut open, or trepanned. As some of the holes show signs of healing, the patients obviously survived the surgery, but nobody knows why it was done. It might have been to relieve pressure on the brain after a blow to the head, or to release the evil spirits which were thought to possess some people.

This skull has been cut open at least four times.

Chapter Seven

Astronomy and calendars

Because the peoples of Peru depended on farming to survive, they needed some means of marking the passing of the seasons so that they could plough their fields and plant their seeds at the correct times. The Inca emperor, Pachacuti, drew up a calendar of 12 months, each divided into 30 days. Simple observatories were also built for the priests to watch the movements of the Sun and the planets. Some consisted of just a single stone pillar whose shadow would allow the priest to measure the movement of the Sun, but others had several pillars with pierced discs on top through which the Sun's rays would pass at different times of year.

A closer look

The single stone pillar for measuring the movement of the Sun was possibly known as an Inti Huatana. This means 'the post where the Sun is tied'. In the winter the Incas watched its shadow carefully, waiting for the moment when the Sun reached the solstice and was at the furthest point from the Inca lands. Religious ceremonies then took place to encourage the Sun to come back and warm the Inca lands once more. In their determination to wipe out all traces of the Inca religion, the Spaniards destroyed every Inti Huatana they found.

The Spaniards never found the Inca stronghold of Machu Picchu – and so its Inti Huatana survived.

ARTS AND CRAFTS

Although many Inca artefacts were stolen or destroyed by the Spaniards in the 16th century, and others have been stolen by grave-robbers in more recent times, enough survive to show us that the Incas and their predecessors were skilled potters, stonemasons and metalworkers. Many items were produced for everyday use, but the most ornate were probably made especially to be buried with the dead, either to show their importance in this life or as offerings to the gods.

SHARED IMAGES

From Chavin times to the defeat of the Inca Empire, all the peoples of Peru used similar images to decorate their pottery and textiles, carvings and metalwork. These images were based on the natural world and on religious ideas. They included jaguars, condors, snakes, eagles, cayman, crocodiles, frogs and humans, and many strange creatures which were made up of the features of two or three different animals or humans. There were also many different versions of the Staff God (see page 15). Some designs from the coastal areas show mountain scenes, while some designs from the mountain areas show the ocean and off-shore islands, suggesting that the various civilisations knew about each other's territory from early times. However, although the same images reappear, they were depicted in different ways at different times. Sometimes they looked realistic, at other times they had geometric shapes or elongated arms and legs, making them harder to recognise.

This Moche pot is in the shape of an imaginary creature with the body of a snake, the head of a deer and the teeth of a large cat.

POTTERY

Pottery was first made in Peru around 2000 BC. Before that date, plant gourds were used as containers for storage and as cups and bowls. But after that date, maize became an increasingly important crop. Maize needed to be cooked in pots so, as this knowledge spread, pottery gradually replaced gourds in everyday use.

Early pottery was either plain or very simply decorated, but by Chavin times designs were carved in low relief or painted on to the pots. The Paracas people cut their designs into the clay, as did the early Nazca people. Later Nazca pottery has multi-coloured designs, and often shows the image of the Strangler, a mythological creature with a long, pointed tongue. Moche pottery was often shaped to represent people, animals and plants. Some pots represented a single human face, but others showed several different figures in action, including battle scenes and hunting scenes, mothers and their children, healers and priests at work and the punishment of criminals and prisoners of war.

Pottery from Tiahuanaco and Huari was painted in many different colours. Chimu pottery was largely mass-produced and mainly black in colour, while the Incas made a full range of items, from painted vases and bowls, to effigy figures and large, patterned water-pots, known as *aryballos*, which were designed so that the water did

The man on this Inca pot is carrying a large water-pot on his back.

ARTS AND CRAFTS

not spill out when the pot was being carried on the back.

All these pots were made without the aid of a fast-spinning potter's wheel. Sometimes the shape was achieved by coiling long strips of clay on top of each other, but some pots were moulded in the hand from a ball of clay. Many effigy pots were made in two halves, by smoothing clay inside two moulds, then removing it just before it dried out and sticking the two parts together. When the pot had been shaped, it was dried in the sun, then painted and finally fired to harden it.

Only an Inca of high status would have been allowed to wear a richly decorated tunic such as this one from the south coast of Peru.

TEXTILES

In ancient Peru, the finest textiles were valued more highly than gold. Textiles were often buried with the dead, not just as clothing, but also as beautifully patterned lengths of cloth to wrap around the mummified body. From the Chavin civilisation to

that of the Incas, cotton and wool from the backs of alpaca and vicuña were spun and woven into good-quality cloth, while wool from llamas was used for items such as ropes and rough blankets.

Textile patterns were created in many different ways. Patterns were woven on the loom by using yarns of different colours. Plain cloth could also be tie-dyed or have patterns painted on to it. The most spectacular designs, however, were those made by the Paracas people for use as burial cloths (see page 8). These cloths had alternating plain and

51

embroidered squares, with no two patterns ever being exactly the same. They showed warriors holding severed heads, priests flying in drug-induced trances, and people dressed as animals. Almost 200 different colours have been counted in the embroidery which was done with needles made from bone or wood, and it has been estimated that each cloth took up to 30 years to complete. These patterns probably related to the dead person's status in life, but other, simpler patterns were also used to distinguish the costumes worn by people from each village or *ayllu*.

A CLOSER LOOK
Most of the dyes for cloth were made from the roots, leaves or flowers of many different plants, but bright red was obtained from the bodies of cochineal insects which had been dried and crushed.

Featherwork garments were worn only for special festivals and ceremonies. As well as the human figure in the centre, this one is patterned with birds and fish.

FEATHERWORK

Cloaks, *ruanas* (ponchos) and tunics for wealthy nobles and rulers were sometimes decorated with patterns made from brightly coloured feathers. The feathers were obtained from wild birds caught in the Amazon rainforests. The garment itself was made from woven cloth with the quills of the feathers pushed through from front to back and fastened in. Thousands of feathers were needed for just one garment. Feathers were also used to make headdresses for nobles and to make fans (see page 36) and whisks to cool the face, or flick flies and insects away.

A CLOSER LOOK

From Chavin times, gold jewellery was worn as a sign of a person's social status. It was made into armlets and bracelets, necklaces and pendants. It was also made into ear-discs which were mainly worn by noblemen and priests. These ear-discs were often decorated with inlaid patterns made from pieces of turquoise or shell, or from coloured feathers. Men had their ears pierced when they were quite young and wore bigger and bigger discs in the hole to stretch it, until it was big enough to push an egg through!

METALWORK

Gold was used in Peru for ornaments and jewellery from at least Chavin times. At first people hammered it into sheets which could be cut or bent into the required shape and decorated with embossed patterns. By Chimu times, however, many more metalworking skills had been mastered. Chimu goldsmiths knew how to weld pieces of gold together, shape cups and dishes around wooden templates, make inlaid and filigree patterns, fix a layer of gold plating on to copper objects and create beautiful ornaments using the lost-wax method. They also used tiny plates of gold to decorate clothes and bags for the very rich. When

Chimu goldsmiths made this mask by beating pieces of gold into shape. Two snarling, cat-like creatures hang upside-down from the axe-shaped headdress.

the Incas conquered the Chimu, they were so impressed with Chimu workmanship that they took the best goldsmiths from Chan Chan to Cuzco to work for the emperor.

MUSIC AND DANCE

Throughout the Inca year, there were many festivals. Some were linked to farming, celebrating a plentiful harvest or a successful sowing of seeds. Others were religious festivals or marked events in the lives of the people in the *ayllus*, such as coming-of-age or marriage ceremonies. Food and drink played an important part at these celebrations, as well as music. Archaeologists have found the remains of panpipes, flutes, drums and even a clay trumpet from Inca times and earlier. A 17th-century drawing by Poma de Ayala (see page 9) shows women singing and beating drums while the men are dressed as birds and getting ready to dance.

This pottery bottle shows a man playing a tune on the panpipes.

STORYTELLING AND HISTORY

With no written language, the peoples of ancient Peru learned stories and history by heart and passed them from one generation to the next by word of mouth. In Inca times, when the Sapa Inca died a council of nobles met and decided which parts of his life should be remembered. These were recorded on *quipus* (see page 30), and people known as rememberers also learned what to say about the dead ruler. Nearly all of this information was lost, however, when most of the *quipus* were destroyed by the Spanish invaders.

CIVIL WAR AND THE DEFEAT OF THE INCAS

Inca history was eventually written down by the Spaniards after the conquest of the Inca Empire. They tell us that in 1525 while the Sapa Inca, Huayna Capac, was trying to extend his empire northwards, he was informed of an epidemic that was sweeping through Cuzco and the surrounding area. He quickly turned south to try and deal with the problem, but reached only as far as present-day Quito before falling ill himself. No one today is sure what the epidemic was, but it seems likely to have been either smallpox or measles. Both these diseases were introduced to South America by the Spaniards who settled around La Plata on the east coast and were probably brought to the Andes area by people who traded with the Spaniards. The native peoples had not encountered these diseases before, so they had no natural resistance to them and large numbers died.

HUAYNA CAPAC'S SUCCESSORS

A CLOSER LOOK

When the Sapa Inca did not have a son by his sister (the Coya), he needed to choose one of his other sons to be Sapa Inca after him. Once he had made his choice, he asked his priest to sacrifice a llama and remove its lungs. A sign on them would then indicate whether the gods approved of the Sapa Inca's choice or not. If they did not, then another son was chosen and the ceremony was repeated.

Huayna Capac's death was sudden and unexpected, and he did not have time to name his successor properly. By tradition it should have been his son by the Coya, but she had no children. In such a case, the Sapa Inca was supposed to choose his successor with the help of divine approval. Huayna Capac had chosen Ninan Cuyuchi who was with him, but Huayna Capac died before the priest could perform the ceremony of approval and Ninan Cuyuchi died shortly afterwards. Huascar, another son who was in Cuzco at the time, was Huayna Capac's next choice and the priest in Quito decided to name him as the next Sapa Inca without any ceremony of approval. This angered Atahuallpa, half-brother to Huascar, who was in Quito with Huayna Capac and his army. Huascar demanded that Atahuallpa return to Cuzco, but Atahuallpa refused. An official was then sent to see him, but Atahuallpa's response was to kill him and have a drum made out of his skin. When the drum was sent to Huascar, civil war broke out between the two brothers and their supporters.

The war lasted until April 1532, when Huascar's army was finally defeated and Huascar himself was taken prisoner. At that time Atahuallpa was at a town called Cajamarca and he ordered Huascar to be brought to him there. Atahuallpa was now Sapa Inca, but his reign was destined to be a short one.

THE SPANIARDS ARRIVE

Since Christopher Columbus had first sailed to the West Indies in 1492, the Spaniards had gradually been building an empire in what they called the 'New World'. The Spanish took control of Mexico in 1521 and over the next ten years groups of adventurers set off both north and south in search of gold and other treasures. One of these groups, led by Francisco Pizarro, landed at Tumbes on the north coast of Peru early in 1532. Pizarro led fewer than 200 men, most of whom were soldiers. They had

A CLOSER LOOK

Francisco Pizarro was born in Spain around 1478 and went to the Spanish colony of Hispaniola (now Haiti and the Dominican Republic) in 1502. He started his explorations of South America in 1510. From 1519 to 1523 he was mayor of Panama, a town which had been founded by the Spaniards. Over the next nine years he went on several more expeditions along the west coast of the continent. On one of these he crossed the Equator and met a raft travelling from Peru with a cargo of embroidered cloth and precious metals. No doubt he also heard that the Inca Empire was being torn apart by civil war and would be relatively easy to conquer.

CIVIL WAR AND THE DEFEAT OF THE INCAS

guns and wore armour and about a third of them were on horseback. By the end of the year, the Inca Empire would be under their control.

THE MEETING AT CAJAMARCA

Poma de Ayala drew this picture of Atahuallpa and Pizarro at Cajamarca almost 90 years after the meeting took place.

After they had defeated Huascar, Atahuallpa's soldiers went to join their leader in a camp at Cajamarca. There they heard stories about the strangers who had landed on the coast and were now heading towards them. Atahuallpa was curious but not afraid, as he had around 50,000 men with him. When Pizarro and his soldiers arrived in Cajamarca they invited Atahuallpa to go and meet them on 16 November 1532. Atahuallpa accepted the invitation. His attendants carried him to the meeting on a golden litter and his bodyguard of around 6000 men went too. Atahuallpa was expecting a peaceful meeting, but Pizarro and his men had prepared an ambush. When Atahuallpa reached the main square of Cajamarca, a Spanish priest stepped forward and started to preach to him, offering him a Bible. Atahuallpa, who had never seen a book before, looked at it carefully then threw it down as it meant nothing to him. The Spaniards took this as a signal to attack and began shooting at the unarmed Incas. Many of them were killed and Atahuallpa was taken prisoner.

THE DEATH OF ATAHUALLPA

Realising that the Spaniards were interested in gold, Atahuallpa offered to fill a room with gold objects in exchange for his freedom. Pizarro agreed, but, when the room was full, he took the treasure and still kept Atahuallpa in prison. While he was being held captive, Atahuallpa ordered the execution of his

CHAPTER NINE

rival, Huascar, to prevent the Spaniards making him Sapa Inca in Atahuallpa's place. Pizarro used this as an excuse to charge Atahuallpa with murder. The Sapa Inca was found guilty and sentenced to be burned to death. Believing that the destruction of his body would prevent him from living again after his death, Atahuallpa finally agreed to accept Christianity in exchange for the promise that he would be strangled to death rather than burned. He was baptised on 29 August 1533 and executed on the same day.

SPANISH RULE

Used to their lives being strictly ruled by the Sapa Inca, the peoples of his empire did not know what to do when he was dead. Though some tried to resist the Spaniards, their weapons were no match for guns and cannons and they were eventually defeated. Their temples were destroyed and their

A CLOSER LOOK

After the death of Atahuallpa, the Spaniards put another of Huayna Capac's sons on the throne as Sapa Inca. His name was Manco Inca, but he was a puppet ruler and had to do what the Spaniards told him. He managed to escape to a remote area called Vitcos, where he set up a small but independent Inca state with its capital at Vilcabamba. This state survived until 1572. Vilcabamba was the city for which the archaeologist Hiram Bingham was looking in 1911 when he discovered the ruins of Machu Picchu.

Manco Inca sitting on his throne

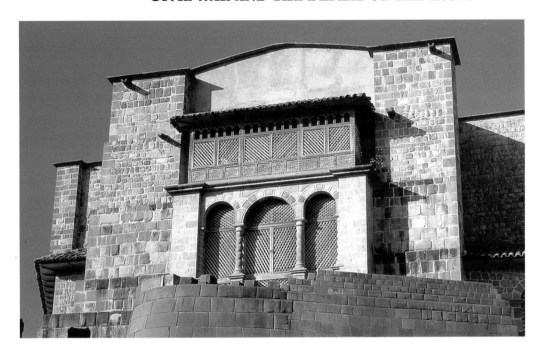

The Christian church of Santa Domingo now stands on the site of Coricancha in Cuzco, but the walls of the old Inca shrine can still be seen in the foreground.

treasures were stolen. Missionaries arrived from Spain to convert them to Christianity and a monastery was built on the site of Coricancha. By 1535 the Spaniards had complete control of Peru. They turned many of its people into slaves and forced them to work in the fields and in the gold and silver mines. The Spaniards did not understand the irrigation systems, and let them fall into ruin. The crops failed, and soon people began to starve to death. Many more were killed by diseases brought from Europe. The Inca people and their civilisation were almost wiped out. But in remote parts some of the old gods and the old traditions were remembered and managed to survive until the 19th century, when the country regained its independence. Though Spanish remains the main language in Peru, and Christianity is the country's main religion, some of the Inca ways are still remembered today, including the Festival of Inti Raymi which celebrates the return of the Sun after the winter solstice.

A CLOSER LOOK

In 1535 Francisco Pizarro founded the city of Lima as the new capital of Peru, and Cuzco lost its earlier importance. Because of his ruthlessness, Pizarro had many enemies amongst the Spaniards and, in June 1541, they joined forces and attacked his palace in Lima. Pizarro was killed but, in 1542, the *conquistadors* chose his half-brother, Gonzalo Pizarro, as the new governor of Peru.

TIMELINE

Note: The earliest accurate date in the history of Peru is 1438 when Pachacuti Inca Yupanqui came to the throne. All the dates before this are based on archaeological evidence and so are approximate, rather than exact.

BC

10,000	People are living in Peru by this date.
8000	Attempts are made to cultivate some plants in the fertile valleys.
6000	Potatoes are cultivated in the highlands.
3000	The first people start to settle on the coast.
2500	People start to settle in the river valleys and in the highlands.
2300	Large-scale building projects start in the river valleys.
2000	Cultivation of maize starts and pottery begins to appear.
1700	The first large ceremonial centres are built.
1000	People start to settle around Tiahuanaco.
900	Possible start of the Chavin civilisation
850	Work begins on the temple complex at Chavin de Huantar.
600	Probable start of the Paracas civilisation
200	Collapse of the Chavin civilisation and start of the Nazca civilisation

AD

1	Start of the Moche civilisation
175	Collapse of the Paracas civilisation
300	The Lord of Sipan is buried.
500	The Tiahuanacan civilisation starts to expand.
600	The start of the Huari civilisation
800	The Nazca and Moche civilisations have collapsed by this date.
900	By this date the Huari civilisation has collapsed and Huari has been abandoned.
1000	Start of the Chimu civilisation
1100	The Tiahuanacan civilisation has collapsed by this date.
1200	Construction of the Chimu capital, Chan Chan, begins. Manco Capac, the first Inca emperor, takes his people to Cuzco and builds his capital city there.
1438	Pachacuti Inca Yupanqui becomes Sapa Inca and greatly expands the Inca Empire.
1471	Topa Inca Yupanqui becomes Sapa Inca and the expansion continues.
1476	The Incas defeat the Chimu and make their lands part of the Inca Empire.
1491	Huayna Capac becomes Sapa Inca.
1525	The Inca Empire is at its greatest extent when Huayna Capac dies.
1532	In April, Atahuallpa defeats his half-brother Huascar and becomes Sapa Inca. The Spaniards, led by Francisco Pizarro, land at Tumbes in northern Peru. In November, Pizarro tricks Atahuallpa and takes him prisoner.
1533	Atahuallpa is executed by the Spaniards on 29 August. The Spaniards make Manco Inca into the new Sapa Inca.
1535	Francisco Pizarro founds Lima as the new capital of Peru.
1537	Manco Inca escapes to Vilcabamba and sets up an independent Inca state.
1541	Francisco Pizarro is killed by his enemies.
1572	Tupac Amaru, one of Manco Inca's sons, becomes the last Sapa Inca. He is captured by the Spaniards and executed. The Inca Empire comes to an end.

GLOSSARY

adobe – bricks made from clay and dried in the sun.

altiplano – a bleak area of high grassland in the Lake Titicaca region of the Andes.

ayllu – a social group based on an extended family structure. It could be as small as a village or as large as a city.

bullion – gold and silver in bars and ingots.

camelid – a member of the camel family. In South America these include the vicuña, llama, alpaca and guanaco.

cassava – a plant. Its roots can be made into a type of flour.

cayman – an alligator.

colony – a group of people who settle in a foreign country.

conquistadors – the Spaniards who conquered Mexico and Peru in the 16th century.

El Niño – the name given to unusually warm ocean conditions which affect the west coast of South America every few years. El Niño can cause devastating storms and floods.

filigree – fine metalwork that looks rather like lace.

hallucinogenic – describes substances such as drugs that cause hallucinations.

huaca – shrines at rocks, springs or caves where people left offerings and made sacrifices.

litter – a seat on poles on which the Sapa Inca was carried by his servants.

mit'a – tax paid with manual labour.

mummies – bodies which have been preserved by drying after death.

oracle – a place where the gods can be asked to give advice or predict the future.

pontoon – a bridge made by fastening boats together and (sometimes) placing planks across them to make a walkway.

puna – high, treeless grassland in the Andes.

puppet ruler – someone who is given the title of ruler, while someone else is really in control.

Quechua – the language spoken by the Incas, and their ancestors.

quinine – a drug from the bark of the cinchona tree used to cure fevers.

quinoa – a high-protein grain that grows at high altitudes.

quipu – a collection of knotted strings used by the Incas for recording numbers and other information.

ruana (**poncho**) – a cloak made of an oblong piece of cloth with a hole in the middle for the head to go through.

Sapa Inca – 'Sole Ruler', the emperor of the Incas.

shaman – a ritual specialist who reads omens, predicts the future and performs ceremonies.

smelting – obtaining metal from ore by means of heating it.

solstice – the day of the year when the sun is directly overhead at either the Tropic of Cancer or the Tropic of Capricorn.

squash – a vegetable rather like a pumpkin or a marrow.

trapezoid – a four-sided figure, like a triangle with the top cut off.

tribute – a set amount of goods given by conquered people to their new rulers, usually in exchange for peace and protection.

trophy head – the head of an enemy taken in battle and kept as proof of victory.

INDEX